Verbal Reasoning
Progress Papers 3

Patrick Berry

Schofield&Sims

Introduction

The **Verbal Reasoning Progress Papers** provide structured activities that increase in difficulty throughout the series, developing your knowledge and skills in verbal reasoning. Use the books to prepare for school entrance examinations and to improve your verbal reasoning skills.

How to use this book

There are six papers in this book. Each contains 100 questions, divided by topic into sets of five. A single paper may take between 45 and 75 minutes to complete, and you might need two or more sessions to complete one paper.

- For exam preparation, revision and all-round practice, you may choose to work through the papers in numerical order. Once you have completed a paper, ask a teacher, parent or adult helper to correct any mistakes and to explain where you went wrong.

- To practise a topic that you find particularly challenging, work through selected activities in order of difficulty using the **Topics chart**, available to download from the Schofield & Sims website.

Answers

The answers to all the questions in this book can be found in a pull-out section in the middle. You (or an adult) should use this to mark your work at the end of each paper. You will receive one mark for each correct answer, giving you a total mark out of 100 for every paper. Take time to learn and remember why the answer given is correct.

Use the **Progress chart** at the back of this book to record your marks and measure progress.

Downloads

Free downloads are available from the Schofield & Sims website (www.schofieldandsims.co.uk/free-downloads), including extra practice material.

Published by **Schofield & Sims Ltd**
7 Mariner Court, Wakefield, West Yorkshire WF4 3FL, UK
Telephone 01484 607080
www.schofieldandsims.co.uk

First published in 2016
This edition copyright © Schofield & Sims Ltd, 2018

Author: **Patrick Berry**
Patrick Berry has asserted his moral rights under the Copyright, Designs and Patents Act, 1988, to be identified as the author of this work.

Grateful thanks to Siân Goodspeed and Denise Moulton for their contribution to **Verbal Reasoning Progress Papers**.

British Library Cataloguing in Publication Data
A catalogue record for this book is available from the British Library.

Design by **Oxford Designers and Illustrators**
Cover design by **Ledgard Jepson Ltd**
Printed in the UK by **Page Bros (Norwich) Ltd**

ISBN 978 07217 1472 1

Contents

Note for parents, tutors, teachers and other adult helpers
A pull-out answers section (pages A1 to A12) appears in the centre of this book, between pages 26 and 27 (Paper 15). This provides answers to all the questions, along with guidance on marking the papers. Remove the pull-out section before the child begins working through the practice papers.

Q. 1–5

sorting
information

Read the information below carefully. Use the information to fill in the table. Then answer the questions.

Some drivers were asked which kinds of car they preferred.

James and Maria preferred estate cars, sports cars and 4×4s. Hannah, Tom and Dave voted for small cars. George and Harry liked sports cars, small cars and people carriers. Maria, Hannah, Rima and Jess liked people carriers. The main preferences for Rima, Jess and George were 4×4s and diesel cars.

	4×4 car	Sports car	People carrier	Estate car	Small car	Diesel car
James						
Maria						
Hannah						
Tom						
Dave						
Harry						
Rima						
Jess						
George						

1   How many preferred three types of car?   _____   1 ☐

2   Who liked the most types of car?   _____   2 ☐

3   How many said they liked people carriers?   _____   3 ☐

4   Who had only one preference?   _____   4 ☐

5   Who liked both sports cars and small cars?   _____   5 ☐

Q. 6–10

letters for
numbers

If **A** is **2**, **B** is **3**, **C** is **5**, **D** is **10** and **E** is **12**, work out these calculations. Give the answer as a letter.

Example B + A = ☐   <u>C</u>

6   A + B + C = ☐   _____   6 ☐

7   E + B = D + ☐   _____   7 ☐

8   (C × A) = ☐   _____   8 ☐

9   E + C + B = A × ☐   _____   9 ☐

10   E ÷ B = (B + C) ÷ ☐   _____   10 ☐

MARK ☐

MARK
✓ OR ✗

Q. 11–15

missing four-letter words

In each of these sentences, the word in CAPITALS has four letters missing. These four letters make a real four-letter word. Write the four-letter word on the line.

Example He was hungry but the food CUPD was empty. _BOAR_

11   I must put a clean PER on my cut finger.   _____   11 ☐

12   The large lorry was pulling a long TER.   _____   12 ☐

13   In the desert the lost explorer was PED and desperate for water.

                                                               _____   13 ☐

14   When the paper is SPED from the walls, we can redecorate. _____   14 ☐

15   My mobile phone contract has FINI so I need to renew it. _____   15 ☐

Q. 16–20

jumbled words in grids

The letters at the bottom of each grid fit into the boxes above them to make **two** words. Work out where each letter goes.

16

a g y i w s n

16 ☐

17

h

t e s e y s h

17 ☐

18

i

b p s s n g i

18 ☐

19

h

r e w w o e h

19 ☐

20

p

a e h y a p p

20 ☐

MARK ☐

MARK
✓ OR ✗

Q. 21–25

spot the word

A four-letter word is hidden in each of these sentences. You will find the hidden word at the end of one word and the beginning of the next. Underline the hidden word and then write it on the line.

Example Daniel ended the speech with a joke.   _lend_

21   It is common sense to avoid eating unripe fruit.

_____   21 ☐

22   Her money-making scheme attracted many investors.

_____   22 ☐

23   The Go-Anywhere ticket also means free travel for a week.

_____   23 ☐

24   He planted hundreds of flowers including some pretty peonies.

_____   24 ☐

25   You must complete the task within the forty-five minutes.

_____   25 ☐

Q. 26–30

analogies

Underline **one** word in the brackets to complete these analogies.

Example Arrive is to depart as come is to (run hurry go train hide).

26   Painting is to artist as book is to (library shelf author printer reader).   26 ☐

27   Hot is to warm as cold is to (green amber icy cool temperature).   27 ☐

28   Dozen is to twelve as decade is to (result gross hundred ten ruin).   28 ☐

29   Grape is to raisin as plum is to (dessert pudding prune fig custard).   29 ☐

30   Leg is to knee as arm is to (thumb wrist thigh hand elbow).   30 ☐

MARK ☐

MARK
✓ OR ✗

Q. 31–35

time problems

Here is part of a train timetable.

Answer the questions using the 24-hour clock.

Departs from Station A	Arrives at Station B
06:15	10:35
08:45	13:05
11:20	15:40
12:55	17:20
13:40	18:10
15:05	19:30

Departs from Station B	Arrives at Station A
06:40	11:10
07:50	12:15
09:25	13:55
10:50	15:25
11:55	16:10
13:40	18:15

31 How many trains in either direction are travelling at noon?

_____   31 ☐

32 A fast train completes the journey to Station A in the quickest time. At what time does it begin its journey from Station B? _____   32 ☐

33 If John leaves A to travel to B on the 08:45 train, what is the earliest time he can arrive back in A?   _____   33 ☐

34 How many trains from A to B complete their journey before six o'clock in the evening?   _____   34 ☐

35 I have to be back at A before 2.00 p.m. What is the latest train I can catch from B in order to be there on time?   _____   35 ☐

Q. 36–40

antonyms

Underline two words, **one** from **each** set of brackets, that have the **opposite** meaning.

Example (happy kind mouth grin)   (smile sad face cheerful)

36 (lenient friendly easy peculiar)   (amiable odd enemy strict)   36 ☐

37 (second hour minute month)   (enormous timely clock exceptional)   37 ☐

38 (serious slight single simple)   (great trivial few upwards)   38 ☐

39 (many frequent falsehood definite)   (untruthful truthful truth often)   39 ☐

40 (scared frightening flee cowardice)   (opinion belong bravery run)   40 ☐

MARK ☐

MARK
✓ OR ✗

Q. 41–45

jumbled words in sentences

The letters of the words in CAPITALS have been mixed up. Write the **two** correct words on the lines.

Example The TERWA was too cold to WSIM in. <u>WATER</u> and <u>SWIM</u>

41 The TRAPCEREN soon repaired the ROOD frame.
_____ and _____

42 Dad used a pair of PERILS to remove the rusty SLAIN.
_____ and _____

43 The RANGED sign warned everyone to PEEK out of the quarry area.
_____ and _____

44 He was a ULCER master and treated his TAVERNS badly.
_____ and _____

45 I have just heard the RUSTLE of the rugby TAMCH.
_____ and _____

41	☐
42	☐
43	☐
44	☐
45	☐

Q. 46–50

word chains

Turn the word on the left into the word on the right in two moves. You can only change one letter at a time. Each change must result in a real word.

Example T A L E <u>TAKE</u> <u>LAKE</u> L I K E

46 M A K E _____ _____ B A R N

47 P O L E _____ _____ T A L K

48 R E A D _____ _____ T O L D

49 S I D E _____ _____ T A M E

50 T A K E _____ _____ L I N E

46	☐
47	☐
48	☐
49	☐
50	☐

Q. 51–55

letter sequences

Write the next two items in each sequence. Use the alphabet to help you.

Example AB CD EF GH <u>IJ</u> <u>KL</u>

A B C D E F G H I J K L M N O P Q R S T U V W X Y Z

51	AY	ZX	YW	XV	WU	VT	_____	_____
52	CD	TS	GH	RQ	KL	PO	_____	_____
53	DI	DE	EA	GW	JS	NO	_____	_____
54	CD	FF	JI	MK	QN	TP	_____	_____
55	GU	IS	KQ	MO	OM	QK	_____	_____

51	☐
52	☐
53	☐
54	☐
55	☐

MARK ☐

Schofield & Sims • Verbal Reasoning Progress Papers 3

MARK
✓ OR ✗

Q. 56–60 complete the sentence	Underline **one** word in **each** set of brackets to make the sentence sensible.

Example The (plumber electrician baker) repaired the (light loaf sink) so that we could (lamp hear see) again.

56 The (infant pilot doctor) carefully guided the (submarine frisbee helicopter) away from the electric (cables cooker toothbrush).

56 ☐

57 The (cowslip cowboy coward) drove the (herd pack set) of (cards bulls butterflies) to the rail depot.

57 ☐

58 The (undertaker chef tailor) prepared a fine (bouquet banquet bucket) for the (monarch monocle monotony).

58 ☐

59 When the famous (diver driver diva) sang a well-known (area arena aria), she received loud applause from the (clapping audio audience).

59 ☐

60 The (detective directive decisive) knew that (frenzied forensic frenetic) (endurance insurance evidence) was very important.

60 ☐

Q. 61–65
word categories

Underline the **general** word in each row, which is the word that includes all the others.

Example banana apple fruit raspberry pear kiwi

61 cayman slowworm reptile iguana chameleon python gecko 61 ☐

62 biplane seaplane turbojet helicopter aircraft gyrocopter 62 ☐

63 major private soldier colonel corporal sergeant lieutenant 63 ☐

64 aunt relative grandmother uncle son father daughter 64 ☐

65 polygon decagon pentagon dodecagon triangle hexagon 65 ☐

Q. 66–70
word connections

Underline the **one** word from the brackets that fits best with the three words at the start.

Example feed eat scoff (hate mock laugh false devour)

66 errand task job (fight homework ironing chore painting) 66 ☐

67 unlocked unbolted unchained (closed open secure shut alarmed) 67 ☐

68 butter yoghurt cream (bread egg cheese meal cow) 68 ☐

69 pupil scholar schoolchild (teacher professor mark clever student) 69 ☐

70 purify decontaminate freshen (cleanse cleaner cleanest cleanliness) 70 ☐

MARK ☐

MARK
✓ OR ✗

Q. 71–75

mixed-up groups

Two groups of three words have been mixed up in each question. Work out which would be the **middle** word in each group if they were in the correct order. Underline these **two** words.

Example city   <u>adolescent</u>   village   <u>town</u>   infant   adult

71	wasp	fifth	seventh	butterfly	sixth	flea	71
72	sandal	puddle	pond	shoe	lake	boot	72
73	branch	onion	splinter	garlic	leek	trunk	73
74	January	vine	December	grape	February	vineyard	74
75	country	green	amber	county	continent	red	75

Q. 76–80

join two words to make one

Circle **one** word from **each** group, which together will make a longer word.

Example (pond (dam) river)   (era down (age))

76	(trick con art)	(joke led trickle)	76
77	(wear some garb)	(era badge body)	77
78	(waste west waist)	(tip turn coat)	78
79	(friend down pal)	(ice ship mate)	79
80	(waist drain smoke)	(pipe gutter water)	80

Q. 81–85

word meanings

Each of these words can have **three** meanings. Write the numbers of the three meanings in the table below.

Example			81			82			83			84			85		
grave			fly			match			port			deliver			green		
3	7	10															

Meanings   1 used to make fire   2 to rush   3 a place for burial
4 to help at a birth   5 a harbour   6 game
7 an accent in French   8 a colour   9 an insect   10 serious
11 without experience or training   12 a computer socket
13 a strong wine   14 to give a speech
15 lawn for playing bowls   16 to move through the air
17 equal with   18 to take post to an address

81

82

83

84

85

MARK

MARK
✓ OR ✗

Q. 86–90 odd ones out	One word in each question does **not** belong with the rest. Underline this word.	
	Example horrid nasty <u>kind</u> mean unfriendly	
86	Berlin London Birmingham Paris Madrid Dublin Edinburgh	86
87	B E S Z K M N	87
88	herd flock shoal school bottle colony pack	88
89	February March May July August October December	89
90	Mercury Jupiter Neptune Zeus Saturn Venus Mars	90

Q. 91–95 rhyming words	Add **one** word to complete each sentence. The word you add must rhyme with the word in CAPITALS.	
	Example TOAD The lorry was carrying a heavy <u>load</u> .	
91	THUMB His fingers were blue and _____ with cold.	91
92	MILE The house was built in the Tudor _____ with wooden beams.	92
93	SLATE I was so late I told my friend not to _____ .	93
94	LANE The _____ of Queen Victoria ended in 1901.	94
95	SOME She was so hungry she ate every last _____ .	95

Q. 96–100 missing letters	The same **two** letters end the first word and begin the next word. Write the letters.	
	Example T R A <u>I</u> <u>L</u> <u>I</u> <u>L</u> L N E S S	
96	F R A __ __ __ __ L E G A L	96
97	P I E R __ __ __ __ N T R E	97
98	S P E __ __ __ __ R I V E	98
99	T R U __ __ __ __ O U G H	99
100	D E __ __ __ __ L O N	100

MARK ☐

PAPER 13 TOTAL MARK ☐

END OF TEST

START HERE

MARK
✓ OR ✗

Q. 1–5

alphabetical order

Number the words in each line in alphabetical order. Use the alphabet to help you.

Example

CAT	CAN	CAR	CAW	CAB	CAP
5	2	4	6	1	3

A B C D E F G H I J K L M N O P Q R S T U V W X Y Z

1 programme profit protect prospect produce promenade
   ☐ ☐ ☐ ☐ ☐ ☐   1 ☐

2 reverberate reveal reverence revere revelation reverie
   ☐ ☐ ☐ ☐ ☐ ☐   2 ☐

3 quiver quadrant quadrangle quadrille quad quadrilateral
   ☐ ☐ ☐ ☐ ☐ ☐   3 ☐

4 sky ski skiing skim skill skincare
   ☐ ☐ ☐ ☐ ☐ ☐   4 ☐

5 practical practice practicable practically practicality practicability
   ☐ ☐ ☐ ☐ ☐ ☐   5 ☐

Q. 6–10

word connections

Underline the **one** word that fits with **both** pairs of words in brackets.

Example (heart club) (ruby emerald) jewel brain <u>diamond</u> card brooch

6 (sphere globe) (dance party) fun reel jig earth ball   6 ☐

7 (excellent beautiful) (fee penalty) good punishment charge fine nice   7 ☐

8 (identical similar) (approve enjoy) eat like same correct taste   8 ☐

9 (indicate show) (purpose reason) comma colon point idea play   9 ☐

10 (clown idiot) (hoodwink deceive) fool trick silly stupid daft   10 ☐

MARK ☐

MARK
✓ OR ✗

Q. 11–15

letters for numbers

If **A** is **1**, **B** is **2**, **C** is **5**, **D** is **10** and **E** is **12**, work out these calculations. Give the answer as a letter.

Example C + C = ▢ <u>D</u>

11 2E + A = ▢ ² _____ 11 ▢

12 E + D – B = 2 × ▢ _____ 12 ▢

13 2C + ▢ = E _____ 13 ▢

14 A + B + C = ▢ – 2 _____ 14 ▢

15 2B + A + C = ▢ _____ 15 ▢

Q. 16–20

mixed-up questions

The words are jumbled up in these questions. Work out what each question is. Then write the **answer** to that question. Put one letter in each box.

Example toes foot? are many How each on | f | i | v | e |

16 relation sister's What your is daughter? you to ▢▢▢▢▢ 16 ▢

17 grown are vineyard? a in What ▢▢▢▢▢▢ 17 ▢

18 which Tower? is In Eiffel city the ▢▢▢▢▢ 18 ▢

19 game at played What is Wimbledon? ▢▢▢▢▢▢ 19 ▢

20 call What number trees? do you a large of ▢▢▢▢▢▢ 20 ▢

Q. 21–25

join two words to make one

Circle **one** word from **each** group, which together will make a longer word.

Example (pond (dam) river) (era down (age))

21 (car part sign) (rage age tune) 21 ▢

22 (walk pal mate) (shop real lid) 22 ▢

23 (fur for back) (vent row word) 23 ▢

24 (should can am) (dell have bush) 24 ▢

25 (yard clothes mile) (stone rock ware) 25 ▢

MARK ▢

MARK ✓ OR ✗

Q. 26–30

word codes

Work out these codes. The code used in each question is different. Use the alphabet to help you.

A B C D E F G H I J K L M N O P Q R S T U V W X Y Z

Example If the code for BUS is DWU, what is the code for COACH? _EQCEJ_

26 If the code for CARROT is DBSSPU, what is the code for CABBAGE?

_____ 26 ☐

27 If the code for PENGUIN is SHQJXLQ, what is the code for BISCUIT?

_____ 27 ☐

28 If the code for ZEBRA is EJGWF, what is the code for POSSIBLE?

_____ 28 ☐

29 If the code for PECULIAR is NCASJGYP, what is the code for STRANGE?

_____ 29 ☐

30 If the code for NAUGHTY is IVPBCOT, what is the code for RUBBISH?

_____ 30 ☐

Q. 31–35

word categories

Below this table are 10 words. Write each word in the correct column.

31	32	33	34	35
Cornwall	Thames	Birmingham	France	Himalayas
Norfolk	Severn	Glasgow	Hungary	Cairngorms

31 ☐
32 ☐
33 ☐
34 ☐
35 ☐

Tyne   Nottingham   Austria   Avon   Cardiff   Kent
Greece   Atlas   Cumbria   Pennines

Q. 36–40

change a letter

Read the clue in brackets. Change **one** letter in the word in CAPITALS to make it match the clue. Write the new word on the line.

Example SANE (alike) _SAME_

36 SMELL (not large)   _____ 36 ☐

37 CRISIS (a potato snack) _____ 37 ☐

38 CHANCE (coins in pocket) _____ 38 ☐

39 GRATE (elegance)   _____ 39 ☐

40 HARROW (a vegetable)   _____ 40 ☐

MARK ☐

MARK
✓ OR ✗

Q. 41–45

rhyming words

Add **one** word to complete each sentence. The word you add must rhyme with the word in CAPITALS.

Example TOAD   The lorry was carrying a heavy __load__ .

41	RIPE	Alfie wasn't the _____ of boy to get into much trouble.	41 ☐
42	KITE	She failed her driving test because her _____ wasn't good enough.	42 ☐
43	TIME	Ravi tried to _____ the tree but it was too difficult.	43 ☐
44	CAUGHT	The pupils _____ they would do well in the spelling test.	44 ☐
45	HATS	Amelia put her hair in _____ before the party.	45 ☐

Q. 46–50

odd ones out

Two words in each question do **not** belong with the rest. Underline these **two** words.

Example horrid   nasty   <u>kind</u>   mean   unfriendly   <u>helpful</u>

46	urban rural pastoral city rustic agricultural countryside	46 ☐
47	scurry hurry dally tarry scuttle scamper hasten	47 ☐
48	prevent aid veto disallow help forbid prohibit	48 ☐
49	detect overlook notice observe behold witness ignore	49 ☐
50	pretty ghastly horrible frightful handsome dreadful awful	50 ☐

Q. 51–55

spot the word

A four-letter word is hidden in each of these sentences. You will find the hidden word at the end of one word and the beginning of the next. Underline the hidden word and then write it on the line.

Example Daniel <u>end</u>ed the speech with a joke.   __lend__

51	If you are clever you will find this hidden word.	_____	51 ☐
52	The ball often went over the fence into Mark's garden.	_____	52 ☐
53	The cheese was eaten by the hungry mice.	_____	53 ☐
54	Eating sugary things may damage tooth enamel.	_____	54 ☐
55	We keep our warm coats on in this cold weather.	_____	55 ☐

MARK ☐

Q. 56–60

antonyms

Underline two words, **one** from **each** set of brackets, that have the **opposite** meaning.

Example (<u>happy</u> kind mouth grin) (smile <u>sad</u> face cheerful)

56	(bandage hurt doctor injury) (heel splint hospitalise heal)	**56**
57	(easy difficult hard simplicity) (different complexity odd add)	**57**
58	(obstacle help barrier friend) (hinder mate carer reef)	**58**
59	(benevolent kind repulsive unfortunate) (attractive happy sad bad)	**59**
60	(defendant judge witness clerk) (prison police plaintiff crime)	**60**

Q. 61–65

symbol codes

The word **ALERTING** is written as ► █ ▲ ♦ ◄ — ▼ ■ in code. Use the same code to work out the hidden words.

61	► █ ◄ ▲ ♦ — ▼ ■ _____	**61**
62	— ▼ ◄ ▲ ■ ♦ ► █ _____	**62**
63	◄ ♦ — ► ▼ ■ █ ▲ _____	**63**
64	♦ ▲ █ ► ◄ — ▼ ■ _____	**64**
65	■ ♦ ▲ ▲ ◄ — ▼ ■ _____	**65**

Q. 66–70

number sequences

Write the next two numbers in each sequence.

Example 2 4 6 8 <u>10</u> <u>12</u>

66	40 39 35 40 30 41 _____ _____	**66**
67	21 16 28 23 35 30 _____ _____	**67**
68	17 18 17 19 18 21 20 _____ _____	**68**
69	20 18 19 16 17 13 14 _____ _____	**69**
70	16 18 21 17 19 22 18 _____ _____	**70**

MARK

MARK
✓ OR ✗

Q. 71–75

word meanings

Each of these words can have **two** meanings. Write the numbers of the two meanings in the table below.

Example		71		72		73		74		75	
organ		great		down		sack		tick		wind	
11	12										

Meanings   1 marvellous   2 the noise of a clock   3 to turn or twist
4 unhappy   5 soft feathers   6 very big
7 a bloodsucking insect   8 a bag   9 movement of air
10 to dismiss   11 a musical instrument   12 part of the body

71 ☐
72 ☐
73 ☐
74 ☐
75 ☐

Q. 76–80

jumbled words in sentences

The letters of the words in CAPITALS have been mixed up. Write the **two** correct words on the lines.

Example The TERWA was too cold to WSIM in.   _WATER_ and _SWIM_

76   Before dinner he set the BLEAT with the best CRUELTY.

_____ and _____   76 ☐

77   After he fell Tomasz had a RUBIES on his GEL.

_____ and _____   77 ☐

78   Megan sat on the OAFS and DARE her book.

_____ and _____   78 ☐

79   At the DEN of the day I go to PEELS.

_____ and _____   79 ☐

80   She RIDES her hands on the OWLET.

_____ and _____   80 ☐

Q. 81–85

change a word

One word is incorrect in each sentence. Underline this word. Write the correct word on the line.

Example Climbing over that wall is not aloud. _allowed_

81   The teacher criticised Grace's poor spilling.   _____   81 ☐

82   The allens came to visit the Earth in their spaceship.   _____   82 ☐

83   Anna went to the salon to have her nails manured.   _____   83 ☐

84   I phoned for an imbalance to take him to hospital.   _____   84 ☐

85   Jakub fell asleep on the haddock that hung between two trees.

_____   85 ☐

MARK ☐

MARK
✓ OR ✗

Q. 86–90

make a word

Look at how the second word is made from the first word in each pair. Complete the third pair in the same way. Write the answers on the lines.

Example (fright rights) (flight lights) (height _eights_)

86	(buts stub)	(rail liar)	(rotavator _____)	86

87 (tribal trial) (stable stale) (timber _____) 87

88 (able bale) (alter later) (arid _____) 88

89 (hear misheard) (behave misbehaved) (manage _____) 89

90 (bring big) (prevail peal) (brittle _____) 90

Q. 91–95

mixed-up groups

Two groups of three words have been mixed up in each question. Work out which would be the **middle** word in each group if they were in the correct order. Underline these **two** words.

Example city adolescent village town infant adult

91 crouch sleep stand doze blink lie 91

92 gobble lane nibble trail highway eat 92

93 pebble growl roar boulder whisper stone 93

94 bookcase apple bookshelf tree library orchard 94

95 wood forest glider aeroplane tree rocket 95

MARK _____

MARK
✓ OR ✗

Q. 96–100

word grids

Fit each set of words into the grid. The words should read across and down.

96

t	a	m	e	s

ridge   taste   armed
coast   cater ~~tames~~

97

i	s	s	u	e

every   probe   paint
tasty   ousts ~~issue~~

98

ladle   reeve   greed
where   tiger   towel

99

chair   opera   enter
above   treat   antic

100

peaty   party   inter
cheap   chimp   extra

96 ☐
97 ☐

98 ☐

99 ☐
100 ☐

MARK ☐

PAPER 14 TOTAL MARK ☐

END OF TEST

Q. 1–5

complete the sentence

Underline **one** word in the brackets to make the sentence sensible.

Example The yacht sailed into the (shop hospital <u>harbour</u> cinema matchbox).

1 She (boat walked slept rowed oozed) across the Atlantic all by herself. | **1** ☐

2 Archie's father's brother is Archie's (mother uncle nephew grandfather stepson). | **2** ☐

3 Beer is made from (hops skips jumps races flies). | **3** ☐

4 The bride of the (broom groom boom bloom loom) wore a beautiful white dress. | **4** ☐

5 In the USA there are one hundred (scents euros dimes quarters cents) in one dollar. | **5** ☐

Q. 6–10

which word

One word in each question **can** be made from the word in CAPITALS. Underline this word. You may only use each letter once.

Example SPEEDBOAT   toast   debated   poems   <u>beast</u>   poser

6	ARTIFICIAL	clear	facial	later	chart	first	**6** ☐
7	CENTIPEDE	descend	dented	decent	pedant	scented	**7** ☐
8	DIFFERENT	deferred	entered	deter	inferred	internal	**8** ☐
9	INTRODUCTION	introduce	reduce	contented	induct	product	**9** ☐
10	CONFERRED	differ	relief	credence	friend	freed	**10** ☐

Q. 11–15

mixed-up sentences

Two words must swap places for each sentence to make sense. Underline these **two** words in each sentence.

Example The <u>bone</u> growled softly as he approached the <u>dog</u>.

11 The belfry in the bell rang at midday today. | **11** ☐

12 Losing her mobile phone was a misery which added to Ava's mystery. | **12** ☐

13 The bus fair to the fare was very expensive. | **13** ☐

14 Without artificial aid water is not possible under breathing. | **14** ☐

15 He had an attack of pins and arms in his needles. | **15** ☐

MARK ☐

MARK
✓ OR ✗

Q. 16–20
spot the
word

A four-letter word is hidden in each of these sentences. You will find
the hidden word at the end of one word and the beginning of the next.
Underline the hidden word and then write it on the line.

Example Daniel <u>ended</u> the speech with a joke.   <u>lend</u>

16   Some flowers repel insects while some attract them.

_____ | 16 ☐

17   The centre of the city really does need a one-way system.

_____ | 17 ☐

18   Our coach informed me that the game had been postponed.

_____ | 18 ☐

19   After a long wait Ping's plane finally arrived four hours late.

_____ | 19 ☐

20   Call your friend and ask him if he's going to the concert.

_____ | 20 ☐

Q. 21–25
rhyming
words

Add **one** word to complete each sentence. The word you add must rhyme
with the word in CAPITALS.

Example TOAD   The lorry was carrying a heavy <u>load</u>.

21   DECEIVE   I could not _____ the news when I heard it on
television. | 21 ☐

22   MINE   At the end of a road is a _____ which tells you
to stop. | 22 ☐

23   LIME   We had sage and _____ stuffing with the turkey. | 23 ☐

24   COW   We attached the swing to an overhanging _____
of the tree. | 24 ☐

25   CUFF   The head teacher told us that she'd had _____
of our bad behaviour. | 25 ☐

MARK ☐

MARK
✓ OR ✗

Q. 26–30
odd ones out

One word in each question does **not** belong with the rest. Underline this word.

Example horrid   nasty   <u>kind</u>   mean   unfriendly

26	dodder	totter	falter	leap	shuffle	stagger	26 ☐
27	hullabaloo	furore	frenzy	tumult	calm	rowdiness	27 ☐
28	compliant	mutinous	rebellious	unruly	revolutionary	riotous	28 ☐
29	easy-going	amiable	placid	amicable	harmonious	aggressive	29 ☐
30	lax	severe	stringent	serious	rigorous	strict	30 ☐

Q. 31–35
analogies

Underline **one** word in each set of brackets to complete these analogies.

Example Arrive is to (<u>depart</u> plane speed) as come is to (run hurry <u>go</u>).

31   Bonnet is to (hood hat wheel) as boot is to (trunk foot sock).   31 ☐

32   Letter is to (writing word stamp) as digit is to (hand subtract number).   32 ☐

33   Enter is to (come door entrance) as leave is to (exit depart go).   33 ☐

34   Triangle is to (three isosceles degrees) as quadrilateral is to (rectangle shape angle).   34 ☐

35   Chain is to (rope link metal) as ladder is to (stair tread rung).   35 ☐

Q. 36–40
synonyms

Underline two words, **one** from **each** set of brackets, that are **similar** in meaning.

Example (large great <u>tiny</u> huge)   (box <u>small</u> hungry crate)

36	(wages wager wags wagon)	(between better best bet)	36 ☐
37	(serve deserve reserve observe)	(noted notice notary notorious)	37 ☐
38	(emote path empathy pathetic)	(compassion compass tune compare)	38 ☐
39	(complicated simple easy complete)	(diffuse complex reflex sample)	39 ☐
40	(pleasant docile doctor doctrine)	(medicine patience meek soon)	40 ☐

MARK ☐

MARK
✓ OR ✗

Q. 41–45

word meanings

Each of these words can have **two** meanings. Write the numbers of the two meanings in the table below.

Example		41		42		43		44		45	
organ		graze		contract		galley		iris		mint	
11	12										

Meanings 1 to get smaller 2 part of the eye 3 a kind of ship
4 where money is made 5 an agreement
6 a kitchen on a ship 7 a flower 8 a slight wound
9 a herb 10 to eat grass 11 a musical instrument
12 part of the body

41 ☐
42 ☐
43 ☐
44 ☐
45 ☐

Q. 46–50

symbol codes

The word EMIGRANTS is written as ■ ✢ ▲ ► █ ▼ ◄ ♦ — in code. Use the same code to work out the hidden words.

46 ✢ ▲ ► █ ▼ ♦ ■   _____   46 ☐

47 — ♦ █ ▼ ◄ ► ■   _____   47 ☐

48 ♦ █ ▼ ▲ ◄ ▲ ◄ ►   _____   48 ☐

49 ✢ ▼ — ♦ ■ █ ▲ ◄ ►   _____   49 ☐

50 — ♦ █ ■ ▼ ✢ ▲ ◄ ►   _____   50 ☐

Q. 51–55

jumbled words in grids

The letters in each grid make **two** eight-letter words. The letters must stay in the same columns. Work out where each letter goes.

Example

p	i	l	g	r	i	m	s
a	n	n	o	u	n	c	e
p	i	n	o	u	n	m	e
a	n	l	g	r	i	c	s

51

s	a	r	a	n	i	e	g
p	t	r	a	d	g	n	r

52

i	m	e	r	a	i	e	g
s	t	i	t	l	t	n	s

51 ☐
52 ☐

53

d	r	e	m	d	i	u	l
t	r	a	a	p	f	n	g

54

p	o	l	i	r	i	c	l
p	a	t	e	t	n	a	s

55

s	a	t	u	t	n	r	l
i	n	l	e	r	a	a	y

53 ☐
54 ☐
55 ☐

MARK ☐

MARK
✓ OR ✗

Q. 56–60

word chains

Turn the word on the left into the word on the right in two moves. You can only change one letter at a time. Each change must result in a real word.

Example TALE <u>TAKE</u> <u>LAKE</u> LIKE

56	F A I L	_____ _____	B I L L	56
57	R O A D	_____ _____	B E N D	57
58	C O D E	_____ _____	D A R E	58
59	B I L L	_____ _____	T A I L	59
60	L O S E	_____ _____	M O L E	60

Q. 61–65

number sequences

Write the next two numbers in each sequence.

Example 2 4 6 8 <u>10</u> <u>12</u>

61	1	8	27	64			_____ _____	61
62	39	51	102	114	228		_____ _____	62
63	3	6	5	10	9	18	_____ _____	63
64	1920	960	320				_____ _____	64
65	2187	729	243	81			_____ _____	65

Q. 66–70

missing three-letter words

In each of these sentences, the word in CAPITALS has three letters missing. These three letters make a real three-letter word. Write the three-letter word on the line.

Example My father SED me a photo of my mother. <u>HOW</u>

66	The river FED into the ocean.	_____	66
67	The teacher told the students to stop their CTERING.	_____	67
68	People who swim a lot often suffer from CP.	_____	68
69	The passenger told the bus driver that he had FORTEN his bus pass.	_____	69
70	Tariq searched FTICALLY for the missing car keys.	_____	70

MARK ☐

MARK
✓ OR ✗

Q. 71–75

letters for numbers

If **A** is **1**, **B** is **2**, **C** is **5**, **D** is **10** and **E** is **12**, work out these calculations. Give the answer as a letter.

Example C + C = ___D___

71 E – D = _____ 71 ☐

72 2D = 4 × _____ 72 ☐

73 E – C = C + _____ 73 ☐

74 D ÷ B = _____ 74 ☐

75 E + B + A = 3 × _____ 75 ☐

Q. 76–80

jumbled words in sentences

The letters of the words in CAPITALS have been mixed up. Write the **two** correct words on the lines.

Example The TERWA was too cold to WSIM in. ___WATER___ and ___SWIM___

76 The LINO roared deafeningly as it chased its PYRE through the jungle.

_____ and _____ 76 ☐

77 The juice from the CHEAP ran down my HINC.

_____ and _____ 77 ☐

78 The TOGA seems content as it SEAT the grass.

_____ and _____ 78 ☐

79 He DESPOT the SETTLER in the postbox.

_____ and _____ 79 ☐

80 The PISTOL said they had flown over all the DESSERT in the world.

_____ and _____ 80 ☐

Q. 81–85

word categories

Below this table are 10 words. Write each word in the correct column.

81	82	83	84	85
laugh	smile	frown	worried	happy

scowl   anxious   smirk   delighted   grin   giggle
guffaw   grimace   nervous   ecstatic

81 ☐
82 ☐
83 ☐
84 ☐
85 ☐

MARK ☐

MARK
✓ OR ✗

Q. 86–90

leftover letters

Make a word from the letters that are left after the first word has been made from the word in CAPITALS.

Example CARNATION   ration   _can_

86	COMPARE come	_____	86 ☐
87	ENIGMA gain	_____	87 ☐
88	FOSTERED fester	_____	88 ☐
89	CREATED cede	_____	89 ☐
90	MISDIRECT cried	_____	90 ☐

Q. 91–95

position problems

Below is a table of children in a school. Read the information and work out which child is in each year. Write the names next to the correct year in the table. Then answer the questions.

Ali, Ben, Cara, Daisy, Ellie and Freddie all go to the same school.

Ali is three years above Cara.

Ellie is above Ali but below Ben.

Daisy is nearer to Cara than Freddie is.

Year	Child's name
Year 6	
Year 5	
Year 4	
Year 3	
Year 2	
Year 1	Cara

91	Who is in Year 2?	_____	91 ☐
92	Who is in Year 3?	_____	92 ☐
93	Who is in Year 4?	_____	93 ☐
94	Who is in Year 5?	_____	94 ☐
95	Who is in Year 6?	_____	95 ☐

MARK ☐

Verbal Reasoning
Progress Papers 3
Answers

Schofield&Sims

Verbal Reasoning Progress Papers 3

Notes for parents, tutors, teachers and other helpers

This pull-out book contains correct answers to all the questions in **Verbal Reasoning Progress Papers 3**, and is designed to assist you, the adult helper, as you mark the child's work. Once the child has become accustomed to the method of working, you may wish to give him or her direct access to this pull-out section.

When marking, put a tick or a cross in the tinted column on the far right of the question page. **Only one mark is available for each question**. Sub-total boxes at the foot of each page will help you to add marks quickly. You can then fill in the total marks at the end of the paper. The total score is out of 100 and can easily be turned into a percentage. The child's progress can be recorded using the **Progress chart** on page 52.

The child should aim to spend between 45 and 75 minutes on each paper, but may need more time, or more than one session, to complete the paper. The child should try to work on each paper when feeling fresh and free from distraction.

How to use the pull-out answers

This booklet contains answers to all the questions in the book, as well as footnotes to help with marking. Where the child has answered a question incorrectly, take time to look at the question and answer together and work out how the correct answer was achieved.

By working through the tests and corresponding answers, the child will start to recognise the clues that he or she should look for next time. These skills can then be put into practice by moving on to the next paper, as the difficulty increases incrementally throughout the series.

When a paper has been marked, notice if there are any topics that are proving particularly tricky. You may wish to complete some targeted practice in those areas, by focusing on that particular topic as it appears in each paper. For example, if a child has struggled with word meanings, but answered all other questions accurately, you may wish to target only word meanings questions in your next practice session. The **Topics chart**, available to download for free from the Schofield & Sims website, makes it easy to tailor practice to the child's individual needs.

Paper 13

1	4
2	George
3	6
4	Tom and Dave
5	Harry and George
6	D
7	C
8	D
9	D
10	A
11	LAST
12	RAIL
13	ARCH
14	TRIP
15	SHED
16	swing	any*
17	these	shy*
18	spins	big*
19	where	who*
20	happy	ape*
21	idea
22	meat
23	some
24	type
25	hint
26	author
27	cool
28	ten
29	prune
30	elbow
31	6
32	11:55
33	18:15
34	4
35	09:25
36	lenient	strict
37	minute	enormous
38	serious	trivial
39	falsehood	truth
40	cowardice	bravery

Paper 13 – continued

41	CARPENTER	DOOR*
42	PLIERS	NAILS*
43	DANGER	KEEP*
44	CRUEL	SERVANT*
45	RESULT	MATCH*
46	MARE	BARE
	or BAKE	BARE
47	PALE	TALE
48	ROAD	TOAD
49	TIDE	TIME
50	LAKE	LIKE
	or LAKE	LANE

Accept any accurate response to word chain questions.

51	US	TR
52	OP	NM
53	SK	YG
54	XS	AU
55	SI	UG
56	pilot helicopter cables
57	cowboy herd bulls
58	chef banquet monarch
59	diva aria audience
60	detective forensic evidence
61	reptile
62	aircraft
63	soldier
64	relative
65	polygon
66	chore
67	open
68	cheese
69	student
70	cleanse
71	wasp	sixth
72	shoe	pond
73	branch	onion
74	January	vine
75	country	amber

Paper 13 – *continued*

76	trick	led	
77	some	body	
78	waist	coat	
79	friend	ship	
80	drain	pipe	
81	2	9	16
82	1	6	17
83	5	12	13
84	4	14	18
85	8	11	15
86	Birmingham		
87	E (only vowel)		
88	bottle		
89	February (28 days)		
90	Zeus		
91	numb*		
92	style*		
93	wait*		
94	reign*		
95	crumb*		
96	IL		
97	CE		
98	AR		
99	TH		
100	NY		

*spellings must be correct

Paper 14

1	3 2 6 5 1 4	
2	3 1 5 4 2 6	
3	6 3 2 5 1 4	
4	6 1 2 4 3 5	
5	3 6 2 5 4 1	
6	ball	
7	fine	
8	like	
9	point	
10	fool	
11	C	
12	D	
13	B	
14	D	
15	D	
16	niece*	
17	grapes*	
18	Paris*	
19	tennis*	
20	forest*	
21	sign	age
22	pal	lid
23	fur	row
24	am	bush
25	mile	stone
26	DBCCBHF	
27	ELVFXLW	
28	UTXXNGQJ	
29	QRPYLEC	
30	MPWWDNC	
31	Cumbria	Kent
32	Tyne	Avon
33	Nottingham	Cardiff
34	Austria	Greece
35	Atlas	Pennines
36	SMALL	
37	CRISPS	
38	CHANGE	
39	GRACE	
40	MARROW	

Paper 14 – continued

41	type*	
42	sight*	
43	climb*	
44	thought*	
45	plaits*	
46	urban	city
47	dally	tarry
48	aid	help
49	overlook	ignore
50	pretty	handsome
51	very	
52	loft	
53	seat	
54	then	
55	pour	
56	hurt	heal
57	simplicity	complexity
58	help	hinder
59	repulsive	attractive
60	defendant	plaintiff
61	ALTERING	
62	INTEGRAL	
63	TRIANGLE	
64	RELATING	
65	GREETING	
66	25	42
67	42	37
68	24	23
69	9	10
70	20	23
71	1	6
72	4	5
73	8	10
74	2	7
75	3	9
76	TABLE	CUTLERY*
77	BRUISE	LEG*
78	SOFA	READ*
79	END	SLEEP*
80	DRIES	TOWEL*

Paper 14 – continued

81	(spilling) spelling*	
82	(aliens) aliens*	
83	(manured) manicured*	
84	(imbalance) ambulance*	
85	(haddock) hammock*	
86	rotavator	
87	timer	
88	raid	
89	mismanaged	
90	bite	
91	crouch	doze
92	lane	eat
93	growl	stone
94	bookcase	tree
95	wood	aeroplane

96 (across) coast tames ridge
(down) cater armed taste

97 (across) probe issue tasty
(down) paint ousts every

98 (across) tiger where ladle
(down) towel greed reeve[†]

99 (across) above treat chair
(down) antic opera enter[†]

100 (across) cheap inter peaty
(down) chimp extra party[†]

*spellings must be correct

[†]across and down words can also be the other way round

Paper 15

1. rowed
2. uncle
3. hops
4. groom
5. cents

6. facial
7. decent
8. deter
9. induct
10. freed

11. belfry — bell
12. misery — mystery
13. fair — fare
14. water — breathing
15. arms — needles

16. meat
17. tyre
18. chin
19. slat
20. ally

21. believe*
22. sign*
23. thyme*
24. bough*
25. enough*

26. leap
27. calm
28. compliant
29. aggressive
30. lax

31. hood — trunk
32. word — number
33. entrance — exit
34. isosceles — rectangle
35. link — rung

36. wager — bet
37. observe — notice
38. empathy — compassion
39. complicated — complex
40. docile — meek

Paper 15 – continued

41. 8   10
42. 1   5
43. 3   6
44. 2   7
45. 4   9

46. MIGRATE
47. STRANGE
48. TRAINING
49. MASTERING
50. STREAMING

51. stranger — parading*
52. imitates — sterling*
53. tramping — dreadful*
54. paternal — politics*
55. internal — salutary*

56. FALL   BALL
    or BAIL   BALL
    or FALL   FILL
57. READ   BEAD
    or READ   REND
58. CORE   CARE
59. BALL   BAIL
    or BALL   TALL
60. HOSE   HOLE
    or POSE   POLE
    or ROSE   ROLE

Accept any accurate response to word chain questions.

61. 125   216
62. 240   480
63. 17   34
64. 80   16
65. 27   9

66. LOW
67. HAT
68. RAM
69. GOT
70. RAN

Paper 15 – *continued*

71	B
72	C
73	B
74	C
75	C

76	LION	PREY*
77	PEACH	CHIN*
78	GOAT	EATS*
79	POSTED	LETTERS*
80	PILOTS	DESERTS*

81	giggle	guffaw
82	smirk	grin
83	scowl	grimace
84	anxious	nervous
85	delighted	ecstatic

86	par *or* rap
87	me
88	do
89	rat *or* tar
90	mist

91	Daisy
92	Freddie
93	Ali
94	Ellie
95	Ben

96	three*
97	actor*
98	cobbler*
99	nephew*
100	prince*

*spellings must be correct

Paper 16

1	side
2	let
3	light
4	ship
5	less

6	ST
7	CH
8	CY
9	HE
10	AT

11	WARNED	LOUD*
12	SLEDGE	SNOW*
13	READ	BOOK*
14	CLEAN	BEDROOM*
15	ROOTS	GARDEN*

16	BLUSH	BLEAT
17	FEAST	EVERY
18	PILOTS	PLAIN
19	CREATE	NIECE
	or CRATER	NICER
20	WINDOW	OWNED

21	treat
22	drain
23	mentor
24	tailor
25	departs

26	false
27	unknown
28	true
29	unknown
30	false

31	MK	KM
32	PS	SU
33	SI	UG
34	FH	FK
35	SV	VY

36	attract	repel
37	cleanse	pollute
38	imprison	liberate
39	bury	exhume
40	show	hide

Paper 16 – *continued*

41	212 miles
42	from Penzance to Perth
43	from Liverpool to Preston
44	128 miles
45	112 miles
46	chart
47	mare
48	murder
49	shame
50	rankle
51	careful conscientious
52	minuscule tiny
53	enemy nuisance
54	sensible sensitive
55	poverty indigence
56	12:10
57	19:30
58	09:45
59	14:00
60	10:45 14:15
61	MOAN MORN
62	FRAY FLAY
63	PORT POST
	or PORT PORE
	or PAST POST
64	BOUT LOUT
	or LOOT LOUT
65	BAWL BAIL
	or BOIL BAIL

Accept any accurate response to word chain questions.

66	GET
67	AIL
68	TIE
69	MEN
70	OIL
71	TRAIL
72	BLISTER
73	DRAG
74	FAIL
75	STYLE

Paper 16 – *continued*

76	cat
77	music
78	illness
79	medication
80	dairy
81	(hear) read*
82	(proffer) prefer*
83	(typhoon) tycoon*
84	(retrieved) retired*
85	(massacre) mascara*
86	host
87	spell
88	down
89	object
90	make
91	carry bray*
92	table blue*
93	plant snow*
94	fresh asks*
95	trick iced*
96	A
97	B
98	D
99	A
100	D

*spellings must be correct

Paper 17

1. pirates
2. grain
3. fusion
4. contained
5. notice

6. CE
7. LE
8. PH
9. GE
10. SH

11. seed
12. ruin
13. ride *or* dire
14. sister *or* resist *or* resits
15. roped *or* pored

16. ROSE HEIGHT*
17. ACHES ROOM*
18. STOOL STORIES*
19. HEART ROARED*
20. STRAY LOST*

21. pupil teacher
22. weaken strengthen
23. horizontal vertical
24. ignorance knowledge
25. generosity avarice

26. 36 49
27. 121 118
28. $101\frac{1}{4}$ $151\frac{7}{8}$
29. 139 203
30. 16 55

31. B
32. C
33. B
34. D
35. C

36. LAME
37. LEAN
38. MANE
39. FORT
40. REED

Paper 17 *– continued*

41. 17:02
42. 01:11
43. 18:37
44. 00:10
45. 23:49

46. (flew) flu*
47. (learned) taught*
48. (layed) laid*
49. (mouldy) molten*
50. (syrup) stirrup(s)*

51. uglier string
52. shark yoghurt
53. bucket rat
54. rucksack shower
55. secondary rattlesnake

56. fuel
57. gas
58. window
59. young
60. tool

61. 9
62. 8
63. 2
64. 12
65. 11

66. STEP SEEP
67. FLOW FLEW
    or BLEW BLED
    or BLEW FLEW
68. CLAM CRAM
69. STUNG SLUNG FLUNG
    or STINK STUNK SLUNK
    or SLING FLING FLUNG
70. GROVE GLOVE CLOVE

Accept any accurate response to word chain questions.

71. TRIANGLE*
72. PROBLEMS*
73. PERSPIRE*
74. FORTRESS*
75. CIRCULAR*

Paper 17 – continued

76 vest
77 dawn
78 neat
79 near
80 herd

81 novel
82 dustbin
83 help
84 meek
85 temporary

86 B
87 D
88 D
89 B
90 C

91 ROUGH
92 ANKLE
93 BRAG
94 CANINE
95 NOUN

96	baked	cake	iced
97	ache	stomach	doctor
98	music	loud	radio
99	paint	bench	sat
100	munched	baked	well

*spellings must be correct

Paper 18

1	FINCH	BLANK
2	GASP	GRAIN
3	MUSE	LOOT
4	PETTY	BROW
5	LUNCH	PAUNCH

6 out
7 anti
8 in
9 after
10 post

11 spread
12 antler
13 dabble
14 miserable
15 grandstand

16 beech spruce sycamore
17 sprout parsnip courgette
18 topside sirloin rump
19 pronoun preposition adjective
20 emerald onyx topaz

21 part
22 mine
23 round
24 snap
25 note

26	part	ridge
27	down	pour
28	pea	nut
29	ring	tone
30	put	rid

31	SPICES	MEALS*
32	TODAY	PRESENT*
33	LOVELY	KITCHEN*
34	DENIED	RING*
35	SILENT	LISTENED*

36 goal
37 hers
38 herb
39 rein *or* uses
40 fort *or* ball

Paper 18 – continued

41	tortoise	volume
42	window	jumper
43	treble	church
44	tablet	verse
45	quarter	youth
46	mouth	ear
47	start	fall
48	smile	frown
49	leather	food
50	foundations	roots
51	clever	pastry*
52	poster	advert*
53	sailor	yachts*
54	hammer	pencil*
55	cuckoo	linnet*
56	SEND	LEND
	or LAND	LEND
57	COIL	COOL
58	PEST	PENT
	or BENT	PENT
59	BROOD BROOM GROOM		
	or BROOD BLOOD BLOOM		
	or BROOD BROOM BLOOM		
60	SLIMS SLAMS SLAYS		

Accept any accurate response to word chain questions.

61	generous	mean
62	advance	retreat
63	different	similar
64	prosperity	poverty
65	comparable	dissimilar
66	B
67	B
68	E
69	E
70	C
71	PH
72	GH
73	SH
74	TH
75	CH

Paper 18 – continued

76	ugly	grotesque
77	enlarge	increase
78	scoundrel	knave
79	ailing	poorly
80	strong	fit
81	cope*
82	bough*
83	scene*
84	shock*
85	blooms*
86	SCOLD	CHAIR
87	CAPER	DRIPS
88	DWELLS	WHOSE
89	FLIGHT	GLOATS
	or FRIGHT	GROATS
90	THREE	SHAVES
91	POINT
92	COMPUTER
93	OSTRICH
94	SQUARE
95	CHAFF
96	08:40	13:06
97	11:45	15:47
98	09:32	16:14
99	12:30	14:16
100	10:31	17:13

*spellings must be correct

This book of answers is a pull-out section from
Verbal Reasoning Progress Papers 3

Published by **Schofield & Sims Ltd**
7 Mariner Court, Wakefield, West Yorkshire WF4 3FL, UK
Telephone 01484 607080
www.schofieldandsims.co.uk

First published in 2016
This edition copyright © Schofield & Sims Ltd, 2018

Author: **Patrick Berry**
Patrick Berry has asserted his moral rights under the Copyright, Designs and
Patents Act, 1988, to be identified as the author of this work.

British Library Cataloguing in Publication Data
A catalogue record for this book is available from the British Library.

Design by **Oxford Designers and Illustrators**
Printed in the UK by **Page Bros (Norwich) Ltd**

ISBN 978 07217 1472 1

MARK
✓ OR ✗

Q. 96–100

mixed-up questions

The words are jumbled up in these questions. Work out what each question is. Then write the **answer** to that question. Put one letter in each box.

Example toes foot? are many How each on ☐ f ☐ i ☐ v ☐ e

96 many has triangle? How a sides ☐☐☐☐☐ 96 ☐

97 What in films starring? call do a you person ☐☐☐☐☐ 97 ☐

98 shoes boots Who and repairs? ☐☐☐☐☐☐ 98 ☐

99 is son? What your brother's relation you to ☐☐☐☐☐ 99 ☐

100 call What queen? the do you of son a ☐☐☐☐☐ 100 ☐

MARK ☐

Q. 1–5
compound words

Write **one** word that can be written **after** each of the words in the question to make a longer compound word.

Example sew dam garb man pass post _age_

1	be	in	out	off	sea	road	_____	1
2	leaf	ring	trip	brace	tab	drop	_____	2
3	moon	head	search	sun	side	star	_____	3
4	war	fellow	lord	scholar	member	apprentice	_____	4
5	help	hope	use	harm	time	taste	_____	5

Q. 6–10
missing letters

The same **two** letters end the first word and begin the next word in each pair. Write the letters.

Example T E A <u>C H</u> <u>C H</u> I L L   P E A <u>C H</u> <u>C H</u> E A T

6	I N V E __ __	__ __ A R C H	F I R __ __	__ __ A R E	6
7	P I N __ __	__ __ I N K	R A N __ __	__ __ A I R	7
8	F A N __ __	__ __ C L I N G	M E R __ __	__ __ C L O N E	8
9	B A T __ __	__ __ E L	C L O T __ __	__ __ A P	9
10	T R E __ __	__ __ T E M P T	C H __ __	__ __ T I R E	10

Q. 11–15
jumbled words in sentences

The letters of the words in CAPITALS have been mixed up. Write the **two** correct words on the lines.

Example The TERWA was too cold to WSIM in.   <u>WATER</u> and <u>SWIM</u>

11 My dad WARDEN me not to play LUDO music in my room.
_____ and _____ | 11 |

12 We had a great time on our LEDGES in the heavy WONS.
_____ and _____ | 12 |

13 I try to DARE a KOOB every week.
_____ and _____ | 13 |

14 Every Saturday I LANCE my BOREDOM.
_____ and _____ | 14 |

15 The TORSO of the tree next door came up in our DANGER.
_____ and _____ | 15 |

MARK [   ]

MARK
✓ OR ✗

Q. 16–20

add a letter

Add the **same** letter to each pair of words in CAPITALS to make two new words. The added letter can go anywhere in the word. Write the two new words on the lines.

Example CASH and BAKE become _CRASH_ and _BRAKE_ .

16 BUSH and BEAT become _____ and _____ . | 16 ☐

17 FAST and VERY become _____ and _____ . | 17 ☐

18 PLOTS and PLAN become _____ and _____ . | 18 ☐

19 CRATE and NICE become _____ and _____ . | 19 ☐

20 WIDOW and OWED become _____ and _____ . | 20 ☐

Q. 21–25

which word

One word in each question **cannot** be made from the word in CAPITALS. Underline this word. You may only use each letter once.

Example AIRPORT rip <u>park</u> trio pair roar

21 ORCHESTRA chest seat chore treat torch | 21 ☐

22 GARDENER grade drain regard near reader need | 22 ☐

23 PREFERMENT refer ferment mentor freer temper | 23 ☐

24 PARLIAMENT mental tailor martin train remain trail | 24 ☐

25 PARADISE drape parade prise dries spear departs | 25 ☐

MARK ☐

MARK
✓ OR ✗

Q. 26–30

sorting information

Read the information below carefully. Tick (✓) true, false or unknown for each statement. Tick **one** only.

Seven children were asked which kinds of sweets they preferred – mints, liquorice, jelly, sherbet and chocolates.

Annie, Daria, Erum and Freya like mints best.
Billy, Carrie, Daria and Erum like liquorice.
All but Annie like chocolates.
Billy, Daria, Erum and Freya don't like sherbet, but like everything else.

		true	false	unknown	
26	Annie likes chocolate.	☐	☐	☐	26 ☐
27	Gemma likes jelly babies.	☐	☐	☐	27 ☐
28	Daria likes chocolates.	☐	☐	☐	28 ☐
29	Annie likes liquorice.	☐	☐	☐	29 ☐
30	No-one likes chocolates.	☐	☐	☐	30 ☐

Q. 31–35

letter sequences

Write the next two items in each sequence. Use the alphabet to help you.

Example AB   CD   EF   GH   <u>IJ</u>   <u>KL</u>

A B C D E F G H I J K L M N O P Q R S T U V W X Y Z

31 ZA   WC   UE   RG   PI   _____   _____   31 ☐

32 AD   DF   FI   IK   KN   NP   _____   _____   32 ☐

33 GU   IS   KQ   MO   OM   QK   _____   _____   33 ☐

34 RP   RS   NV   NY   JB   JE   _____   _____   34 ☐

35 AD   DG   GJ   JM   MP   PS   _____   _____   35 ☐

MARK _____

Schofield & Sims • Verbal Reasoning Progress Papers 3

MARK
✓ OR ✗

Q. 36–40 antonyms	Underline two words, **one** from **each** set of brackets, that have the **opposite** meaning.	
	Example (<u>happy</u> kind mouth grin) (smile <u>sad</u> face cheerful)	

36	(pretty attract beautiful attractive)	(repel dislike lovely smart)	36 ☐
37	(dirty ugly foul cleanse)	(disgusting pollute scrub disinfect)	37 ☐
38	(decide imprison warder guard)	(defend arrest liberate stand)	38 ☐
39	(bury interest interval grave)	(serious exhume exalt interrogate)	39 ☐
40	(mayday describe show limit)	(restrain control hide hinder)	40 ☐

Q. 41–45

interpreting tables

This chart shows the distance in miles between various cities in the UK.
Use it to answer the questions.

Leeds
73	Liverpool

73	Liverpool												
40	35	Manchester											
91	152	128	Newcastle										
172	215	185	255	Norwich									
65	95	70	152	125	Nottingham								
160	150	141	242	138	94	Oxford							
375	340	342	465	390	320	250	Penzance						
235	251	251	150	400	295	390	590	Perth					
310	275	276	400	320	252	180	78	525	Plymouth				
56	30	31	122	212	100	170	361	225	302	Preston			
33	72	38	122	142	37	125	346	266	280	68	Sheffield		
222	215	204	312	190	157	65	217	454	145	232	191	Southampton	
190	195	181	272	112	121	56	280	416	210	212	160	76	London

41	What is the distance from Norwich to Preston? _____ miles	41 ☐
42	Which is the longest journey on the chart?	
	from _____ to _____	42 ☐
43	Which is the shortest journey on the chart?	
	from _____ to _____	43 ☐
44	How far is it from Newcastle to Manchester? _____ miles	44 ☐
45	How many miles is the return journey from Oxford to London?	
	_____ miles	45 ☐

MARK ☐

MARK
✓ OR ✗

Q. 46–50

make a word

Look at how the second word is made from the first word in each pair. Complete the third pair in the same way. Write the answers on the lines.

Example (fright rights)   (flight lights)   (height _eights_)

46	(sort short)	(sipping shipping)	(cart _____)	46 ☐
47	(shatter share)	(potter pore)	(matter _____)	47 ☐
48	(grub burger)	(cart tracer)	(drum _____)	48 ☐
49	(sale lease)	(last stale)	(mash _____)	49 ☐
50	(stab table)	(lamb amble)	(frank _____)	50 ☐

Q. 51–55

odd ones out

Two words in each question do **not** belong with the rest. Underline these **two** words.

Example horrid nasty <u>kind</u> mean unfriendly <u>helpful</u>

51	clumsy inept careful careless awkward conscientious incompetent	51 ☐
52	large minuscule gargantuan huge tiny immense big	52 ☐
53	associate enemy partner comrade accomplice nuisance colleague	53 ☐
54	ridiculous preposterous silly daft sensible sensitive ludicrous	54 ☐
55	poverty luxury opulence indigence affluence splendour grandeur	55 ☐

Q. 56–60

time problems

Here is part of a bus timetable.

Fill in the missing times using the information given below.

Cardiff to Newport takes 25 minutes.
Newport to Monmouth takes 40 minutes.
Monmouth to Gloucester takes 45 minutes.
Gloucester to Cheltenham takes 15 minutes.

56	Cardiff	08:40		19:05	56 ☐
57	Newport	09:05	12:35		57 ☐
58	Monmouth		13:15	20:10	58 ☐
59	Gloucester	10:30		20:55	59 ☐
60	Cheltenham			21:10	60 ☐

MARK ☐

MARK
✓ OR ✗

Q. 61–65

word chains

Turn the word on the left into the word on the right in two moves. You can only change one letter at a time. Each change must result in a real word.

Example TALE __TAKE__ __LAKE__ LIKE

61	M O A T	_____ _____	T O R N	61
62	T R A Y	_____ _____	F L A T	62
63	P A R T	_____ _____	P O S E	63
64	B O O T	_____ _____	L O U D	64
65	B O W L	_____ _____	B A I T	65

Q. 66–70

missing three-letter words

In each of these sentences, the word in CAPITALS has three letters missing. These three letters make a real three-letter word. Write the three-letter word on the line.

Example My father SED me a photo of my mother. __HOW__

66	Sophie is a VEARIAN and doesn't eat meat.	_____	66
67	It is extremely dangerous to walk on RWAY lines.	_____	67
68	He was a PANT in our local hospital for three weeks.	_____	68
69	In England laws are passed by members of PARLIAT.	_____	69
70	When our gas BER broke down we had no hot water.	_____	70

Q. 71–75

change a letter

Read the clue in brackets. Change **one** letter in the word in CAPITALS to make it match the clue. Write the new word on the line.

Example SANE (alike) __SAME__

71	FRAIL (a path)	_____	71
72	BLUSTER (a bubble on the skin)	_____	72
73	DRUG (pull)	_____	73
74	SAIL (not to succeed)	_____	74
75	STILE (fashion)	_____	75

MARK [ ]

MARK
✓ OR ✗

Q. 76–80 word categories	Underline the **general** word in each row, which is the word that includes all the others.

Example banana   apple   <u>fruit</u>   raspberry   pear   kiwi

76	Cheshire cat tabby tom Siamese puss moggy tortoiseshell	76 ☐
77	overture symphony music chorale concerto hymn pop jazz	77 ☐
78	illness mumps malaria flu polio measles cholera rabies	78 ☐
79	sedative antibiotic linctus tonic antacid steroid medication	79 ☐
80	milk cheese yoghurt dairy cream buttermilk butter whey	80 ☐

Q. 81–85 change a word	**One** word is incorrect in each sentence. Underline this word. Write the correct word on the line.

Example Climbing over that wall is not <u>aloud</u>.   <u>allowed</u>

81	Each day I hear the latest stories in my newspaper. _____	81 ☐
82	Of the three paintings I proffer Nathan's. _____	82 ☐
83	A wealthy typhoon paid for the new hospice. _____	83 ☐
84	Grandpa is retrieved on a pension. _____	84 ☐
85	Isabel uses massacre on her eyes. _____	85 ☐

Q. 86–90 word connections	Underline the **one** word that fits with **both** pairs of words in brackets.

Example (heart club) (ruby emerald)   jewel brain <u>diamond</u> card brooch

86	(angels multitude) (presenter entertainer) many host chat guest crowd	86 ☐
87	(period time) (formula enchantment) charm go magic recipe spell	87 ☐
88	(feathers plume) (below diminish) under down eider pillow cellar	88 ☐
89	(goal purpose) (article item) score object aim match clothing	89 ☐
90	(brand style) (create cook) chef computer do fashion make	90 ☐

MARK ☐

MARK
✓ OR ✗

Q. 91–95

jumbled words in grids

The letters at the bottom of each grid fit into the boxes above them to make **two** words. Work out where each letter goes.

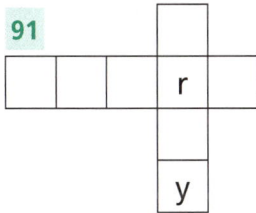

r b y a a c r y

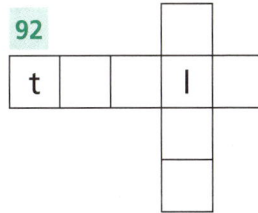

t l b b a e e u

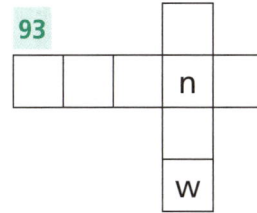

t a r s o w l p

91 ☐
92 ☐
93 ☐

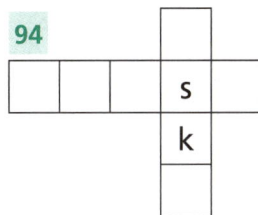

h s e k r f a s

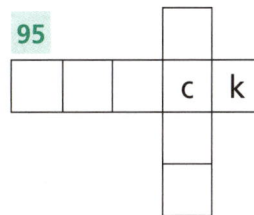

t r i d e k i e

94 ☐
95 ☐

Q. 96–100

letters for numbers

If **A** is **1**, **B** is **2**, **C** is **5**, **D** is **10** and **E** is **12**, work out these calculations. Give the answer as a letter.

Example $C + C = $ ☐   <u>D</u>

96 $C^2 - 2E = $ ☐ _____ 96 ☐

97 $D^2 - 8E = 2 \times $ ☐ _____ 97 ☐

98 $C^2 + B^2 + A = 3 \times $ ☐ _____ 98 ☐

99 $C + B^2 = D - $ ☐ _____ 99 ☐

100 $C^2 + 2E + A = 5 \times $ ☐ _____ 100 ☐

MARK ☐

PAPER 16 TOTAL MARK ☐

END OF TEST

Q. 1–5
which word

One word in each question **can** be made from the word in CAPITALS. Underline this word. You may only use each letter once.

Example SPEEDBOAT   toast   debated   poems   <u>beast</u>   poser

1   PERSPIRATION   spiral   pirates   spinner   nation   notional   spring | 1 ☐

2   HAMMERING   grimy   emerging   murmuring   granary   grain | 2 ☐

3   OBFUSCATION   cross   occasion   counter   fusion   scathing | 3 ☐

4   CONTAMINATED   container   detail   domination   contained   minor | 4 ☐

5   DISCRETION   create   secret   nation   notice   discrete   notion | 5 ☐

Q. 6–10
missing
letters

The **same two** letters end the first word and begin the next word in each pair. Write the letters.

Example T E A <u>C H</u>   <u>C H</u> I L L   P E A <u>C H</u>   <u>C H</u> E A T

6   S I N __ __   __ __ L E R Y   O N __ __   __ __ M E N T | 6 ☐

7   A R T I C __ __ __   __ __ __ A R N   T W I N K __ __ __   __ __ __ A P T | 7 ☐

8   G R A __ __ __   __ __ __ R A S E   E P I T A __ __ __   __ __ __ A N T O M | 8 ☐

9   S T O D __ __ __   __ __ __ A R   B U D __ __ __   __ __ __ N T L E | 9 ☐

10   W A __ __ __   __ __ __ A M E   M E __ __ __   __ __ I N E | 10 ☐

Q. 11–15
leftover
letters

Make a word from the letters that are left after the first word has been made from the word in CAPITALS.

Example CARNATION   ration   <u>can</u>

11   DEPLETES   pelt   _____ | 11 ☐

12   FURNISHER   fresh   _____ | 12 ☐

13   INSERTED   sent   _____ | 13 ☐

14   PERSISTING   ping   _____ | 14 ☐

15   EAVESDROP   save   _____ | 15 ☐

MARK ☐

MARK
✓ OR ✗

Q. 16–20
jumbled words in sentences

The letters of the words in CAPITALS have been mixed up. Write the **two** correct words on the lines.

Example The TERWA was too cold to WSIM in.   _WATER_ and _SWIM_

16   Jack's beanstalk SORE to a great EIGHTH.

_____ and _____   16 ☐

17   When my head CHASE I have to lie down in a dark MOOR.

_____ and _____   17 ☐

18   As a child I sat on my TOOLS and listened to Gran's amazing ROSIEST.

_____ and _____   18 ☐

19   His EARTH beat quickly when the lion ADORER loudly.

_____ and _____   19 ☐

20   Sometimes the sheep TRAYS and get SLOT in the hills.

_____ and _____   20 ☐

Q. 21–25
antonyms

Underline two words, **one** from **each** set of brackets, that have the **opposite** meaning.

Example (happy kind mouth grin)   (smile sad face cheerful)

21   (pupil tutor school uniform)   (eye stutter teacher classroom)   21 ☐

22   (strive improve benefit weaken)   (attempt strengthen try tire)   22 ☐

23   (upright flat horizontal bent)   (vertical smooth down asleep)   23 ☐

24   (brainy ignorance clever wise)   (smart bright lazy knowledge)   24 ☐

25   (mean generosity greedy poor)   (poverty avarice money broke)   25 ☐

Q. 26–30
number sequences

Write the next two numbers in each sequence.

Example 2   4   6   8   _10_   _12_

26   14   8   21   15   28   22   35   29   42   _____   _____   26 ☐

27   170   160   151   143   136   130   125   _____   _____   27 ☐

28   20   30   45 $67\frac{1}{2}$ _____   _____   28 ☐

29   4   13   29   54   90   _____   _____   29 ☐

30   9   1   19   4   30   9   42   _____   _____   30 ☐

MARK ☐

MARK
✓ OR ✗

Q. 31–35
true
statements

Read the information in each question. Circle the **only** statement (A, B, C or D) that has to be true, based on this information.

31 A sparrow is a bird. All birds have feathers.

    A Sparrows lay eggs.

    B Sparrows have feathers.

    C All birds can fly.

    D All birds lay eggs.

31 ☐

32 A lion is an animal. A lion is a carnivore.

    A A cow is a carnivore.

    B All lions have cubs.

    C A lion eats meat.

    D All animals are carnivores.

32 ☐

33 A cabbage is a vegetable. Cabbage is good for you.

    A All cabbages are green.

    B Eating cabbage is healthy.

    C All potatoes are green.

    D Potatoes grow above ground.

33 ☐

34 A cereal is a grain used as food.

    A Soap operas are cereals.

    B All foods are cereals.

    C Barley is a serial.

    D A cereal is food.

34 ☐

35 The Romans invaded Britain against fierce opposition. They built homes with central heating and many roads. They spoke a language called Latin.

    A All British people spoke Latin.

    B All our roads were built by Romans.

    C When the Romans first arrived in Britain they were not welcome.

    D Every home was centrally heated.

35 ☐

MARK ☐

MARK
✓ OR ✗

Q. 36–40

missing four-letter words

In each of these sentences, the word in CAPITALS has four letters missing. These four letters make a real four-letter word. Write the four-letter word on the line.

Example He was hungry but the food CUPD was empty. _BOAR_

36 The judge said that the accident wasn't the driver's fault and he was entirely BLESS. _____ | 36 ☐

37 All the hospital staff were told to insist on hygiene and CLINESS at all times. _____ | 37 ☐

38 The opposite of temporary is PERNT. _____ | 38 ☐

39 The new shoes fitted well and were very COMABLE. _____ | 39 ☐

40 In Roman times, good and loyal slaves were often given their FOM.
_____ | 40 ☐

Q. 41–45

time problems

The times shown on these 24-hour digital clocks are either fast or slow. Write the correct times in the blank clocks. Use 24-hour clock times.

Correct time

41 This clock is 22 minutes slow. | 1 | 6 | 4 | 0 | | | | | | | 41 ☐

42 This clock is 14 minutes slow. | 0 | 0 | 5 | 7 | | | | | | | 42 ☐

43 This clock is 26 minutes fast. | 1 | 9 | 0 | 3 | | | | | | | 43 ☐

44 This clock is 13 minutes slow. | 2 | 3 | 5 | 7 | | | | | | | 44 ☐

45 This clock is 24 minutes fast. | 0 | 0 | 1 | 3 | | | | | | | 45 ☐

MARK ☐

MARK
✓ OR ✗

Q. 46–50

change a word

One word is incorrect in each sentence. Underline this word. Write the correct word on the line.

Example Climbing over that wall is not <u>aloud</u>. <u>allowed</u>

46 Olivia's dad had a bad attack of the flew. _____ | 46 ☐

47 The teacher learned him many interesting things.

_____ | 47 ☐

48 The chicken layed an egg in the barn every morning.

_____ | 48 ☐

49 Mouldy rock flowed down the sides of the erupting volcano.

_____ | 49 ☐

50 She climbed on to the horse's back using the syrup.

_____ | 50 ☐

Q. 51–55

mixed-up groups

Two groups of three words have been mixed up in each question. Work out which would be the **middle** word in each group if they were in the correct order. Underline these **two** words.

Example city <u>adolescent</u> village <u>town</u> infant adult

51	rope	uglier	ugly	thread	string	ugliest	51 ☐
52	milk	shark	yoghurt	whale	butter	trout	52 ☐
53	vole	barrel	fox	bucket	rat	jug	53 ☐
54	drizzle	suitcase	downpour	rucksack	pouch	shower	54 ☐
55	secondary	earthworm	anaconda	tertiary	primary	rattlesnake	55 ☐

Q. 56–60

word categories

Underline the **general** word in each row, which is the word that includes all the others.

Example banana apple <u>fruit</u> raspberry pear kiwi

56 gas petrol oil wood coal kerosene paraffin fuel | 56 ☐

57 oxygen nitrogen gas helium air hydrogen argon | 57 ☐

58 skylight dormer leaded window fanlight sash bay sliding | 58 ☐

59 young calf gosling cub leveret puppy fawn tadpole | 59 ☐

60 wrench spanner hammer tool saw plane drill sander | 60 ☐

MARK ☐

MARK
✓ OR ✗

Q. 61–65

position problems

This is a section of Calvin Road. All the houses are numbered. Some of the children who live in the road are named on the diagram.

From the information given, work out the answers to the questions.

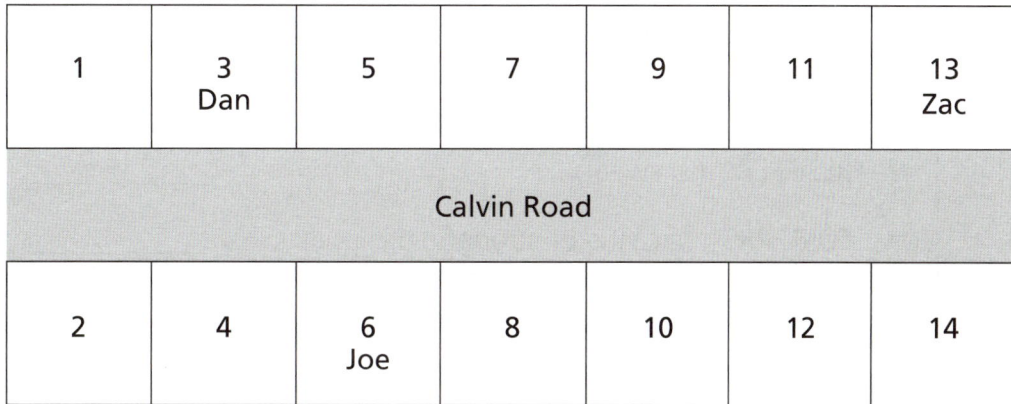

1	3 Dan	5	7	9	11	13 Zac

Calvin Road

2	4	6 Joe	8	10	12	14

61 Adam lives two doors away from Zac in a house with a square number.

Adam lives at number _____ . **61** ☐

62 Shazia lives three doors down from the person who lives opposite Zac.

Shazia lives at number _____ . **62** ☐

63 Zac's furthest neighbour on his side of the road is Bobby, who lives opposite Mia.

Mia lives at number _____ . **63** ☐

64 Kareena lives two doors from Shazia but not opposite Dan.

Kareena lives at number _____ . **64** ☐

65 Dan lives four doors down from Kareena's opposite neighbour Alice.

Alice lives at number _____ . **65** ☐

Q. 66–70

word chains

Turn the word on the left into the word on the right in two moves. You can only change one letter at a time. Each change must result in a real word.

Example T A L E _TAKE_ _LAKE_ L I K E

66 S T O P _____ _____ K E E P **66** ☐

67 B L O W _____ _____ F L E D **67** ☐

68 C L A W _____ _____ P R A M **68** ☐

69 S T I N G _____ _____ _____ F L U N K **69** ☐

70 G R A V E _____ _____ _____ C L O N E **70** ☐

MARK ☐

MARK
✓ OR ✗

Q. 71–75

jumbled words with clues

Each question has a word in CAPITALS. The letters in this word have been mixed up. Use the clue to work out what the word is. Write it on the line.

Example NIBOR   (a bird)   <u>ROBIN</u>

71	GAINLERT (has 180 degrees)	_____	71 ☐
72	SOPBLERM (difficulties to be overcome)	_____	72 ☐
73	RESIPPER (to sweat)	_____	73 ☐
74	FOSTERRS (a castle or stronghold)	_____	74 ☐
75	LARRICUC (shaped like a ring)	_____	75 ☐

Q. 76–80

spot the word

A four-letter word is hidden in each of these sentences. You will find the hidden word at the end of one word and the beginning of the next. Underline the hidden word and then write it on the line.

Example Daniel <u>end</u>ed the speech with a joke.   <u>lend</u>

76	I must remember to buy new gloves tomorrow.	_____	76 ☐
77	That jackdaw nearly flew off with Claire's engagement ring.	_____	77 ☐
78	Looking in the fruit basket I noticed that the peach had been eaten.	_____	78 ☐
79	We must determine around what time the performance should start.	_____	79 ☐
80	A stranger approached her desk and asked for a form.	_____	80 ☐

Q. 81–85

odd ones out

One word in each question does **not** belong with the rest. Underline this word.

Example horrid   nasty   <u>kind</u>   mean   unfriendly

81	newspaper gazette journal novel periodical newsletter	81 ☐
82	junk rubbish trash garbage dustbin debris leftovers	82 ☐
83	nuisance pest irritant plague annoyance burden help	83 ☐
84	meek overbearing imperious arrogant haughty egotistic	84 ☐
85	everlasting temporary eternal permanent immortal undying	85 ☐

MARK ☐

MARK
✓ OR ✗

Q. 86–90

letters for numbers

If **A** is **3**, **B** is **7**, **C** is **8**, **D** is **10** and **E** is **12**, work out these calculations. Give the answer as a letter.

Example A + B = ☐   _D_

86 2D = 4 × ☐ – C   _____

87 5E = 6 × ☐   _____

88 10C = 8 × ☐   _____

89 3E ÷ A = 5 + ☐   _____

90 B² + A² = 2 + B × ☐   _____

86	☐
87	☐
88	☐
89	☐
90	☐

Q. 91–95

crosswords

Look at the clues. Write the answers in the crossword.

91 **1 across** Rhymes with snuff and means coarse.

92 **2 down** Hand is to wrist as foot is to _____?

93 **3 across** If FLOW becomes WOLF, then GARB becomes _____?

94 **4 across** A dog or a tooth.

95 **5 down** A part of speech: any person, place or thing.

91	☐
92	☐
93	☐
94	☐
95	☐

Q. 96–100

complete the sentence

Underline **one** word in **each** set of brackets to make the sentence sensible.

Example The (plumber electrician baker) repaired the (light loaf sink) so that we could (lamp hear see) again.

96 Theo (found boiled baked) a (rabbit cake teaspoon) and then (made blew iced) it.

97 Sajid had a/an (ache pane tooth) in his (shoe stomach hair) and went to see the (circus chiropodist doctor).

98 The (music sun grass) was too (loud hot green) so I switched off the (radio hairdryer cooker).

99 The (cat paint pudding) on the (bench wardrobe jacket) was wet when I (sat danced flew) on it.

100 Toby (munched built threw) the freshly (boiled washed baked) bread and didn't feel (pink well water) afterwards.

96	☐
97	☐
98	☐
99	☐
100	☐

MARK ☐

PAPER 17 TOTAL MARK ☐

END OF TEST

Q. 1–5

move a letter

Take one letter from the first word and put it in the second word to make two new words. Write the two new words on the lines.

Example LIME and ZOO become ___LIE___ and ___ZOOM___ .

1	FLINCH and BANK become	_____ and _____ .	1 ☐
2	GRASP and GAIN become	_____ and _____ .	2 ☐
3	MOUSE and LOT become	_____ and _____ .	3 ☐
4	PRETTY and BOW become	_____ and _____ .	4 ☐
5	LAUNCH and PUNCH become	_____ and _____ .	5 ☐

Q. 6–10

compound words

Write **one** word that can be written **in front** of each of the words in the question to make a longer compound word.

Example work side man guard wood ___fire___

6	side	bid	building	cast	set	door	_____	6 ☐
7	dote	climax	social	septic	inflammatory		_____	7 ☐
8	tend	ability	firm	crease	put	fringe	_____	8 ☐
9	wards	shave	math	shock	glow	noon	_____	9 ☐
10	age	box	card	code	script	graduate	_____	10 ☐

Q. 11–15

which word

One word in each question **cannot** be made from the word in CAPITALS. Underline this word. You may only use each letter once.

Example AIRPORT rip <u>park</u> trio pair roar

11	PROMISED	prods	spread	drops	prose	spire	11 ☐
12	PLEASANTLY	antler	plate	peasant	slant	stale	12 ☐
13	ENABLED	bleed	dean	blend	dabble	need	13 ☐
14	MISERABLY	able	sable	blames	smile	miserable	14 ☐
15	UNDERSTANDING	staring	gears	retains	reading	grandstand	15 ☐

MARK ☐

MARK
✓ OR ✗

Q. 16–20

word categories

Below this table are 15 words. Write each word in the correct column.

16	17	18	19	20
oak	marrow	brisket	verb	garnet
yew	spinach	steak	noun	opal

pronoun   beech   spruce   emerald   topside   sycamore   sirloin   onyx
sprout   rump   preposition   topaz   parsnip   courgette   adjective

16 ☐
17 ☐
18 ☐
19 ☐
20 ☐

Q. 21–25

word meanings

In the centre of each grid, write **one** word which has **all four** meanings given in the grid.

Example

	amusements	
pretty	*fair*	honest
	good weather	

21

	actor's role	
a piece		separate
	to go away	

22

	belonging to me	
colliery		a kind of explosive
	dig underground	

23

	a game of golf	
circular		a slice of bread
	a bullet	

24

	brief spell of weather	
speak angrily		a photo
	a card game	

25

	a part of music	
money		to record
	a short letter	

21 ☐
22 ☐
23 ☐
24 ☐
25 ☐

Q. 26–30

join two words to make one

Circle **one** word from **each** group, which together will make a longer word.

Example (pond (dam) river)   (era   down (age))

26 (core   car   part)   (ridge   rage   drive)

27 (down   jug   rain)   (pore   below   pour)

28 (pea   out   cow)   (some   nut   hard)

29 (cur   ring   car)   (circle   tone   rage)

30 (woe   put   care)   (tea   full   rid)

26 ☐
27 ☐
28 ☐
29 ☐
30 ☐

MARK ☐

MARK
✓ OR ✗

Q. 31–35

jumbled words in sentences

The letters of the words in CAPITALS have been mixed up. Write the **two** correct words on the lines.

Example The TERWA was too cold to WSIM in.   <u>WATER</u> and <u>SWIM</u>

31 Herbs and PISCES make LAMES more flavoursome.

_____ and _____

| 31 | |

32 TOADY is my birthday and my parents gave me a marvellous SERPENT.

_____ and _____

| 32 | |

33 I made a VOLLEY meal in the THICKEN.

_____ and _____

| 33 | |

34 The thief INDEED stealing the GRIN.

_____ and _____

| 34 | |

35 The room was TINSEL as we TINSELED to him recite his poem.

_____ and _____

| 35 | |

Q. 36–40

spot the word

A four-letter word is hidden in each of these sentences. You will find the hidden word at the end of one word and the beginning of the next. Underline the hidden word and then write it on the line.

Example Daniel <u>end</u>ed the speech with a joke. <u>lend</u>

36 I broke my leg and had to forego all hope of playing in the team.

_____

| 36 | |

37 Your hard work will be rewarded by promotion and a higher salary.

_____

| 37 | |

38 The feather bed was more comfortable than all the others.

_____

| 38 | |

39 The fire inside the house showed no sign of abating.

_____

| 39 | |

40 For the opening of Tutankhamun's tomb all the world waited eagerly.

_____

| 40 | |

MARK _____

MARK
✓ OR ✗

Q. 41–45
mixed-up groups

Two groups of three words have been mixed up in each question. Work out which would be the **middle** word in each group if they were in the correct order. Underline these **two** words.

Example city <u>adolescent</u> village <u>town</u> infant adult

41	snail	series	tortoise	volume	page	hare	41 ☐
42	letterbox	shirt	coat	window	jumper	door	42 ☐
43	quadruple	treble	cathedral	double	church	chapel	43 ☐
44	laptop	line	tablet	poem	mobile	verse	44 ☐
45	quarter	child	half	adult	eighth	youth	45 ☐

Q. 46–50
analogies

Underline **one** word in **each** set of brackets to complete these analogies.

Example Arrive is to (<u>depart</u> plane speed) as come is to (run hurry <u>go</u>).

46 Talk is to (gossip mouth whisper) as listen is to (shout hear ear). 46 ☐

47 End is to (final conclusion start) as rise is to (jump high fall). 47 ☐

48 Happiness is to (pleasure gladly smile) as unhappiness is to (dislike frown grin). 48 ☐

49 Cobbler is to (wood leather metal) as chef is to (kitchen food meet). 49 ☐

50 House is to (bricks ceiling foundations) as tree is to (branches roots leaves). 50 ☐

Q. 51–55
jumbled words in grids

The letters in each grid make **two** six-letter words. The letters must stay in the same columns. Work out where each letter goes.

Example

d	r	i	v	e	r
w	a	r	d	e	n
d	a	i	v	e	n
w	r	r	d	e	r

51

c	a	e	v	r	r
p	l	s	t	e	y

52

a	o	s	e	e	t
p	d	v	t	r	r

51 ☐
52 ☐

53

s	a	c	l	t	r
y	a	i	h	o	s

54

h	e	n	m	e	l
p	a	m	c	i	r

55

c	i	c	n	o	t
l	u	n	k	e	o

53 ☐
54 ☐
55 ☐

MARK ☐

MARK
✓ OR ✗

Q. 56–60

word chains

Turn the word at the top of each grid into the word at the bottom. You can only change one letter at a time. Each change must result in a real word.

Example

T	A	L	E
T	A	K	E
L	A	K	E
L	I	K	E

56

S	A	N	D
L	E	A	D

57

B	O	I	L
C	O	O	K

58

B	E	S	T
P	I	N	T

59

B	R	O	A	D
G	L	O	O	M

60

S	L	I	M	E
S	T	A	Y	S

56 ☐

57 ☐

58 ☐

59 ☐

60 ☐

MARK ☐

MARK
✓ OR ✗

Q. 61–65

antonyms

Underline two words, **one** from **each** set of brackets, that have the **opposite** meaning.

Example (<u>happy</u> kind mouth grin) (smile <u>sad</u> face cheerful)

61 (generous familial meaning general) (pleasant mean enemy captain) | 61 ☐

62 (advance country continent content)   (continue retinue retreat go) | 62 ☐

63 (differ same letter different)   (fight oppose correspondent similar) | 63 ☐

64 (prosperity rich poor claim)   (benefit poverty advantage grow) | 64 ☐

65 (likeness compare equal comparable) (match alike dissimilar worthy) | 65 ☐

Q. 66–70

letters for numbers

If **A** is **1**, **B** is **2**, **C** is **5**, **D** is **10** and **E** is **12**, work out these calculations. Give the answer as a letter.

Example $C + C = $ ☐ $\underline{D}$

66 $D \times C = 4E + $ ☐   _____ | 66 ☐

67 $4D = 3E + (2 \times $ ☐ $)$ _____ | 67 ☐

68 $60 = 5 \times $ ☐   _____ | 68 ☐

69 $C^2 = 1 + (2 \times $ ☐ $)$ _____ | 69 ☐

70 $C^2 - 2D = $ ☐   _____ | 70 ☐

Q. 71–75

missing letters

The same **two** letters end the first word and begin the next word in each pair. Write the letters.

Example T E A <u>C H</u> <u>C H</u> I L L   P E A <u>C H</u> <u>C H</u> E A T

71 G R A __ __   __ __ O T O   T R I U M __ __   __ __ O N E | 71 ☐

72 C O U __ __   __ __ O S T   T H O U __ __ __   __ __ __ A S T L Y | 72 ☐

73 F L A __ __   __ __ I N E   M A __ __ __   __ __ O U T | 73 ☐

74 B A __ __ __   __ __ A T   W R A __ __ __   __ __ E M E | 74 ☐

75 F E T __ __   __ __ O I R   M U __ __   __ __ A I R | 75 ☐

MARK ☐

MARK
✓ OR ✗

Q. 76–80

synonyms

Underline two words, **one** from **each** set of brackets, that are **similar** in meaning.

Example (large full great tiny huge)   (box barge small hungry crate)

76	(genial ugly final loose brave) (tight finale gentle beauty grotesque)	76
77	(enlarge fool deceive decrease nod) (aroma increase receive lose fail)	77
78	(dire imagine exact scoundrel know) (navel naval knave knives knew)	78
79	(praise condemn spoil dome ailing) (poorly frighten miss go intend)	79
80	(weak strong week feeble hollow) (strange quiet fit vacant sure)	80

Q. 81–85

rhyming words

Add **one** word to complete each sentence. The word you add must rhyme with the word in CAPITALS.

Example TOAD   The lorry was carrying a heavy __LOAD__ .

81	SOAP	She wasn't sure she could _____ on a desert island.	81
82	COW	The _____ that was hanging off the tree looked dangerous.	82
83	MEAN	The next _____ in the play is the longest.	83
84	KNOCK	The allergic reaction was so severe that he went into _____ .	84
85	FLUMES	The _____ at the flower show were stunning.	85

Q. 86–90

add a letter

Add the **same** letter to each pair of words in CAPITALS to make two new words. The added letter can go anywhere in the word. Write the two new words on the lines.

Example CASH and BAKE become __CRASH__ and __BRAKE__ .

86	SOLD and HAIR become	_____ and _____ .	86
87	CAPE and DIPS become	_____ and _____ .	87
88	DELLS and HOSE become	_____ and _____ .	88
89	FIGHT and GOATS become	_____ and _____ .	89
90	TREE and SAVES become	_____ and _____ .	90

MARK [   ]

Paper 18 • Page 8

MARK
✓ OR ✗

Q. 91–95
word codes

Work out these codes. The code used in each question is different. Use the alphabet to help you.

A B C D E F G H I J K L M N O P Q R S T U V W X Y Z

Example If DWU is the code for BUS, what does EQCEJ mean? _COACH_

91 If OGTKV is the code for MERIT, what does RQKPV mean?

_____ 91 ☐

92 If NNCHMD is the code for MOBILE, what does DNNOVSFQ mean?

_____ 92 ☐

93 If VEFFMX is the code for RABBIT, what does SWXVMGL mean?

_____ 93 ☐

94 If ROGXLDJB is the code for TRIANGLE, what does QNSXPB mean?

_____ 94 ☐

95 If DSVZG is the code for WHEAT, what does XSZUU mean?

_____ 95 ☐

Q. 96–100
time problems

This train timetable shows four train journeys from Alpha to Epsilon, stopping at Beta, Gamma and Delta.

Fill in the missing times using the information given below.

It takes 25 minutes to travel between Alpha and Beta. Alpha to Epsilon takes 1 hour 51 minutes. Beta to Gamma takes 27 minutes. Delta to Epsilon takes 41 minutes. To get to Delta from Gamma takes 18 minutes.

96	Alpha		11:20		15:22
97	Beta	09:05		13:31	
98	Gamma		12:12	13:58	
99	Delta	09:50			16:32
100	Epsilon		13:11	14:57	

96 ☐
97 ☐
98 ☐
99 ☐
100 ☐

END OF TEST

MARK ☐

PAPER 18 TOTAL MARK ☐

Progress chart

Write the score (out of 100) for each paper in the box provided at the bottom of the chart. Then colour in the column above the box to the appropriate height to represent this score.

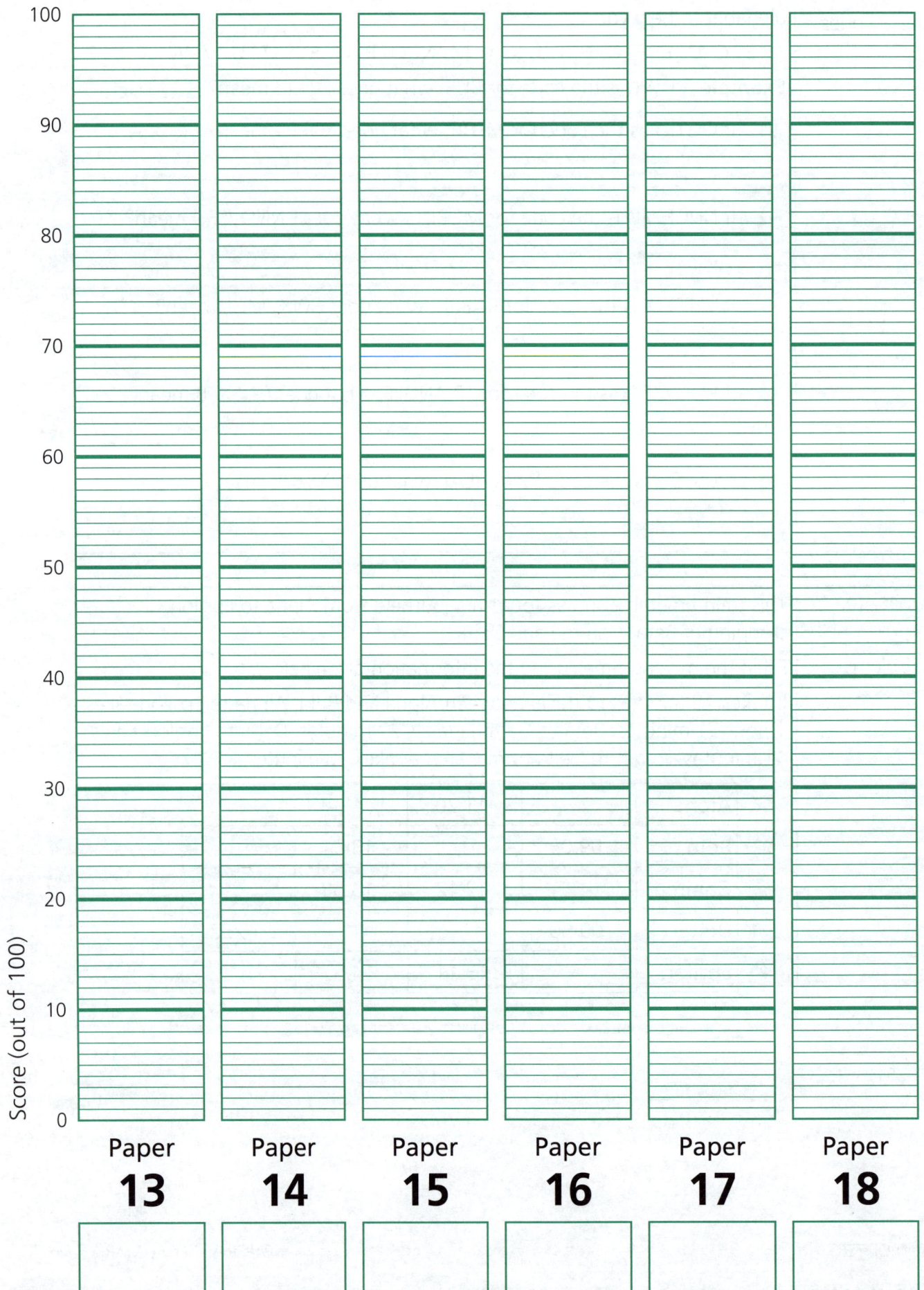

Score (out of 100)

100
90
80
70
60
50
40
30
20
10
0

Paper 13	Paper 14	Paper 15	Paper 16	Paper 17	Paper 18